D1442098

COMMUNICATING WITH **CONFIDENCE**™

BEING A LEADER

ORGANIZING AND INSPIRING A GROUP

JERI FREEDMAN

ROSEN
PUBLISHING®

New York

Published in 2012 by The Rosen Publishing Group, Inc.
29 East 21st Street, New York, NY 10010

Copyright © 2012 by The Rosen Publishing Group, Inc.

First Edition

Library of Congress Cataloging-in-Publication Data

Freedman, Jeri.
Being a leader: organizing and inspiring a group/Jeri Freedman.—1st ed.
    p. cm.—(Communicating with confidence)
Includes bibliographical references and index.
ISBN 978-1-4488-5521-6 (library binding)—
ISBN 978-1-4488-5631-2 (pbk.)—
ISBN 978-1-4488-5632-9 (6-pack)
1. Leadership—Juvenile literature. I. Title.
HM1261.F74 2012
158'.4—dc22

                                                              2011013703

Manufactured in the United States of America

CPSIA Compliance Information: Batch #W12YA: For further information, contact Rosen Publishing, New York, New York, at 1-800-237-9932.

CONTENTS

INTRODUCTION

What is a leader? A leader is a person who has the ability to guide a group of people toward a goal. Some leaders are in positions of authority, such as Boy Scout troop leaders and captains of sports teams. However, many are not, such as those who are working with a volunteer group or school club. Leaders can make people want to work toward a goal without necessarily having the power to order them to perform. Leaders have qualities that make people want to follow them and abilities that allow them to manage people successfully.

A leader is a person who has a vision, an idea of how things can be, and the drive and commitment to achieve that vision. A leader is more than a visionary, however. A leader needs to be able to organize people and resources to make a vision a reality. Being a leader requires perseverance, the ability to keep working toward a goal despite obstacles. Above all, a leader must have excellent communication skills, both written and verbal. How leaders communicate is a key part of what makes them successful. A leader must be articulate, able to speak

For this science project to be successful, the group's leader must make sure each person knows what he or she needs to do and is motivated to do his or her part.

clearly and effectively. A leader must be able to communicate with group members in a variety of situations and ways. A leader must be able to express his or her vision and must be able to clarify for others what his or her role is and what needs to be done to achieve the group's goals. In addition, he or she must be able to talk to members of the group in a way that motivates them to believe in the group's goals and work toward achieving them.

Developing leadership abilities makes one more successful not only in a work setting but also in any setting where one is faced with working with others and accomplishing projects. These can be school projects or school clubs; political campaigns, charities, and social action activities and groups, such as Students Against Drunk Driving (SADD); a part-time job; fund-raising activities such as flea markets, yard sales, or car washes; or neighborhood projects.

Even "natural" leaders were not born that way. They learned and developed the qualities that make them successful. They may have learned them from their parents, by observation, or through their personal experiences, but the fact is that they did learn how to develop those qualities, and you can, too. This book explains the qualities that make a person a leader, as well as how to develop these qualities and use them to successfully manage groups and achieve goals. Being a leader is not easy. It requires a lot of energy and dedication and the ability to deal with people and problems. However, the rewards of developing these abilities are great. The qualities that make one a leader can allow you to realize your goals and those of groups you are involved in. They can make you more successful in school, in sports or a part-time job, and in activities that matter to you, including clubs or charities. They can also make you more successful in future activities, such as college or a career.

THE QUALITIES OF A LEADER

L eadership is about people. Achieving the goals of the group requires motivating people, and motivating people requires understanding them. This chapter discusses the qualities that are important to understanding, communicating with, and leading people.

The Ability to Listen

It's easy to assume that it's what a leader says that is important. Although this is true, to a large extent what is more important is a leader's ability to listen. People want to know their concerns and ideas are being heard.

People are willing to follow a person who listens to them because this makes them feel valued. Good listening skills are important to keeping a group functioning successfully as well. Listening allows a leader to hear issues that are arising both among the members of the group and within the project. In this way, the leader can address problems before they become so large, they are difficult to deal with. Good listening skills allow a leader to better understand group members and other people the group interacts with and to tap into ideas that may improve the project or provide solutions to problems.

Distractions make it difficult to listen to what others are saying. Some distractions are environmental, such as noise. Others are internal, such as worrying about something else when you should be listening or being influenced by personal biases or negative feelings about the speaker. Good listeners learn how to concentrate on the person speaking and avoid distractions during conversations.

Having good listening skills allows a leader to gather ideas from others in the group. Paying attention to what others say encourages them to open up and contribute to the project.

The Ability to Communicate

It is critical for a leader to be able to communicate well. There are many elements to communication. Verbal communication, body language, and attitude all play a role in communication.

Being able to express oneself effectively helps in gaining support not only from peers but also from adults, such as community leaders.

Good communication is well planned, clear, to the point, and easy to follow. Start by thinking about who the audience is. Is it group members, who speak the same language about the subject at hand? School officials? Local businesspeople from whom you are trying to obtain sponsorship or donations? Next, outline your key points so that you can cover them in an organized fashion that will be clear to your audience. Make sure that the language you use is appropriate for the audience to whom you are speaking. When you talk to an audience of community members, your language should be more formal than when talking to your peers. Regardless of your audience, your language should be grammatically correct. This helps get your points across clearly and without ambiguity. Avoid using jargon when you communicate. Jargon consists of specialized terms used within a particular group, hobby, business, industry, or field of study. The meaning of these terms may not be clear to those outside the group, so they hinder rather than help communication.

When you and other group members get together, you may be casual in dress, language, and attitude. However, whenever you have to make a presentation to others or meet with people whose help your group is seeking, you should be careful to dress neatly and present yourself in a respectful, polite manner. People who look professional are simply taken more seriously. Presenting yourself this way also helps people focus on what you're saying rather than being distracted by your clothes, hair, and the like.

When you communicate, body language can be just as important as what you say. Body language includes your facial expressions and gestures, as well as how you stand and move. If you look bored or arrogant, people will be more likely to react negatively to what you say. If you appear open, relaxed, and friendly, they will be more likely to react positively. If you stand with your arms crossed, this can make you look defensive. Standing up straight, instead of slouching or leaning on things, can make you look confident and in control. Make eye contact with the people you are talking to. This both indicates you are focused on them and helps keep them focused on you. Become aware of your body language and use it to your advantage.

Don't forget that other people can become distracted by environmental factors or internal concerns when listening to you. Verify that the people to whom you are speaking got your message correctly by asking them to give you their understanding of what you said or what you requested. If you are speaking to a group, ask for questions at the end of your talk so that you can clarify points that may have been misunderstood or that require further information.

How you write, as well as what you write, influences how others view you, especially words that are broadcast to a large number of people such as tweets on Twitter.

Learn to write clearly and correctly. As a leader, you will have to do a lot of writing—reports, proposals, press releases on the activities of your organization, flyers, and more. The rules of grammar are to language what standards are to computer programming. They allow communication to take place between people clearly and with a minimum of confusion. Take a course in English grammar or read a book on composition, such as *The Elements of Style* by

Active Listening Techniques

Like other leadership skills, good listening techniques must be learned and require practice. Many people think they are good listeners, but most are not. For example, in a discussion, it's common to become distracted by thinking about what one wants to say in response to the other person, instead of listening to him or her. It's common to think one understands what the other person means when that's not the case. There is a series of learned behaviors, called active listening techniques, that can improve your ability to hear and understand what others are saying. Better listening and understanding can reduce confusion and enhance the efficiency of the group. Here is a list of these techniques:

1. Pay attention to the speaker: look directly at the person speaking, not at other things or people in the room. Listen to his or her words, rather than thinking about how you want to respond.

2. Indicate to the other person that you are listening, by means of gestures, nods, or verbalizations such as "Right" or "Mm-hm."

3. Confirm that you understand what the speaker is saying: paraphrase what the speaker has said to ensure that you understand correctly. Ask questions if you're not sure of the speaker's meaning.

4. Let the speaker complete his or her statement before responding: don't interrupt the speaker to argue. Let him or her finish, and then state your counterargument or comment.

5. Respond respectfully: when leading groups, you will sometimes be faced with people who are saying things you disagree with or feel are inappropriate. Be honest in your response, but do not belittle the speaker. An abusive response will make you look bad to other people and make them less likely to be open with you.

William Strunk Jr. and E. B. White. When you are preparing written communication, it is important to plan what you want to say before you begin. If you are writing a lengthy communication, it's often best to outline what you want to cover before you start. To keep your communication clear, express one idea per paragraph. Whenever possible, use the active voice (X did Y, not Y was done).Make sure your communication is concrete, and if you want people to take specific action, convey that clearly. Make sure you proofread anything you write or have a friend check it over for you. It makes you look sloppy and unprofessional to give people written communications that contain typos. Don't rely on the spell-checker to proof your work. It will not find mistakes such as missing words or homonyms (words that sound alike but have different spellings and meanings, such as "whole" and "hole"). The spell-checker also will not catch instances where you typed the wrong word, such as "not" instead of "now" because the incorrect word is spelled correctly.

Today, much communication with the members of a group takes place through electronic media such as e-mail and social media like Twitter and Facebook. Remember that communicating via electronic media is just like communicating on television. You must assume that everyone in the world can see your communication. For this reason, it is of paramount importance that you think before you communicate via electronic means and that you show sensitivity to the feelings of others, both the members of the group and those the group deals with. It is also important to remember that personal information and photos you post on social media sites could ultimately be seen by anyone anywhere. Even if you limit your friends list, members could provide a link to a photo or other information or repeat information you have posted. Your image as a person and a leader will, therefore, be affected by what you post, so think before you post and practice the same rules for good communication and respect on electronic media that you would in verbal or print communications.

The Ability to Bring People Together

By definition, being a leader means being able to bring people together to accomplish a goal. This is one of the most difficult and rewarding tasks of a leader. People who join groups often come from a variety of backgrounds and even different cultures. They have had different experiences and have

A leader must create an atmosphere in which all group members feel comfortable contributing, which means getting people to respect one another's differences.

different types of personalities. It is the leader's job to make the group a hospitable place for all present and potential members and to make sure that everyone feels comfortable contributing to it.

It is up to the leader to create an environment where everyone feels his or her ideas are welcome. Make sure that when ideas are discussed, everyone has a chance to contribute. Do not let some members monopolize discussions or shoot other people's ideas down before they have a chance to express them fully. Ask for contributions from those who are shy. Above all, insist that all team members treat each other with respect while in the group. Do not let stronger members bully weak ones or pick on people who are different. Make it clear that such behavior is inappropriate for a group trying to work together to accomplish a goal. When possible, have different types of people work together. As people get to know one another, they are likely to become more comfortable with one another.When planning the tasks required to complete projects, assign individuals according to their abilities and skills. Make people feel valued. Everyone can contribute something to a project, even if it is packing and moving boxes. If you become accomplished at identifying the sorts of tasks that people are suited for, they will feel they are making a contribution and will work better with other members of the group. If other people give you ideas or suggestions, follow up with them and give them feedback. Doing so makes people feel that their contributions are welcome and that you are willing to consider them.

The Ability to Make People Believe in Themselves

To be a successful leader, you need to trust others. This may seem contradictory, but the fact is that a leader makes other people feel empowered. This, in turn, makes them more willing to take on responsibility, and more work gets done. In some ways, trust is a very difficult skill to learn. You may think you can organize, plan, and execute a task better than anyone else. In some cases, this may be true; in other situations, people may surprise you. However, in most cases, the task will get done and the person doing it will be eager to do more in the future. People need to be trusted, valued, and appreciated. There is no shortcut for doing this.

Evaluate the members' individual skills and talents, and assign them to tasks that are appropriate—then let them get the job done. You must show the group members that you legitimately respect and trust them by not micromanaging or constantly checking on the details of how they're accomplishing their tasks. Instead, plan regular times to meet individually or as a group to review the progress that is being made. At that time, you can address any problems and help people with their tasks.

When problems arise, don't place blame on particular people or let others do so. Instead, approach problems and mistakes as something the team must address and fix together. Make it clear that the success of the project and the whole team depends on their working together to resolve the issue.

If people feel they won't be blamed, they will be more likely to bring up problems sooner, which will provide more time to solve them. When people accomplish their tasks, be sure you tell them they've done a good job and show that you appreciate their efforts.

Self-Discipline

One of the earmarks of a leader is self-discipline. Self-discipline is managing yourself to accomplish what you need to do. This often means applying yourself to work for your group when you'd rather be doing something more fun. Even though doing what you should do isn't as amusing as doing what you want to do, self-discipline pays off in the long run by making you the type of person others can rely on to get things done. This in turn can make you successful in personal, school, and work activities.

In order to succeed in managing yourself, you must be organized and follow through. It is often helpful to map out what your goals are and then make a step-by-step plan for how you plan to accomplish them. This process basically consists of breaking down large goals into small tasks that must be done and giving each task a priority so that you can do the most important ones first. You may then find it helpful to develop a schedule for performing particular tasks that shows when they must be finished. A "to do" list makes it easy to see what needs to be done each day. Many people today keep track of such activities on their smartphone or computer, but paper works fine for this purpose, too!

Keeping a list of what you need to do and checking off items as you accomplish them helps ensure that everything gets done. It also allows you to prioritize activities.

Empathy

As may be apparent from the preceding sections, the key to leading people is understanding them. Good leaders have an abundance of empathy. Empathy is the ability to see through the eyes of another person and feel things as he or she would.

Empathy allows you to understand what other people are feeling. It helps you address the fears and concerns of group members before they become large problems.

It is the ability to put yourself in someone else's place and see yourself or a situation from that person's point of view. This is an invaluable skill because it gives you a unique ability to understand what others are feeling. Understanding how others feel and see things helps you reassure them, encourage them, and instruct them more effectively. It also allows you

to understand what motivates them. For example, some people wish to be stars and thrive on the chance to show off their skills. Some people like to work alone and find that the challenge of solving a problem is its own reward. Some people are highly social and work best as part of a team where they can interact with others. Empathy also lets you sense if someone feels left out or overburdened, which can help you address potential problems before they get out of control.

The Rewards of Being a Leader

It may seem easier to sit back and let others take charge of activities and events. However, stepping up and being a leader has both emotional and practical rewards. There is nothing like the satisfaction of achieving a goal, whether it improves people's lives or results in the success of your team. Achieving goals and helping others achieve them also improves your self-confidence. Once you make a plan, motivate people, and achieve a goal, you know you can do so again.

Being a leader has practical benefits as well. In the process of leading while you are young, you will develop skills that will serve you later in the workplace. Potential employers and college admissions personnel know this, too. Being a successful leader can provide you with a list of concrete achievements that can be put on a résumé or college application.

MYTHS
and
facts

MYTH
Being in charge makes you a leader.

fact
Being elected or put in charge of a group gives you the authority to lead; being a leader requires the ability to make people want to follow you. Many leaders, such as Gandhi, had no position of authority at all.

MYTH
Your followers are there to support you.

fact
The role of the leader is to make the group successful, not the reverse.

MYTH
How you behave outside the group doesn't affect your leadership role.

fact
How group members see you depends on their perception of all your behavior, whether they observe you within the group or in your daily life. If they have a negative impression of you outside the group, this will carry over when they are working with you.

CHAPTER 2

VISION AND GOALS

A key to succeeding as a leader is the ability to inspire others, to make others believe in a vision, and to work toward achieving it. The first step is to develop a vision. The next step is to establish the concrete goals necessary to make the vision a reality. This applies to any project, whether it is raising money for a club, organizing in support of a cause you believe in, or successfully completing a project at work.

Developing a Vision

A vision is something you can imagine the group achieving. A vision is a goal that is larger than one person can achieve alone. A vision can be based on personal desire, for example, a wish for your team or club to win a national championship. Alternately, it can be based on seeing a need and desiring to fill it. For example, you might want to start a shelter for stray dogs and cats, get a referendum on recycling on your town's ballot, or see a particular candidate win a national election. Regardless of motivation, great leaders have vision. They can imagine how things could be. Just think of Martin Luther King Jr.'s "I Have a Dream" speech, which inspired many to believe that there could be equal rights for black people. All great leaders have a compelling vision. Why is having a vision so important? First, a leader is competing for the attention and commitment of people. A compelling vision helps make people feel challenged and enthusiastic. Second, it clarifies what the group is trying to achieve. In order to get where one is going, one has to know where that is. A vision also holds the group together and keeps them focused when obstacles arise. A vision inspires people, and often the larger the vision, the more inspiring it is. People need to feel that they are working for something important and meaningful.

Communicating a Vision

To obtain the commitment of group members, it's imperative to communicate the vision clearly and in a way that attracts, excites, and challenges people. Good communication doesn't just happen. To communicate your vision clearly, you need to plan what you want to say and organize your key points so that you can express them to others. One key aspect of communicating a

People often want to work for a meaningful goal. The key to enrolling them in a cause is communicating a vision of what could be accomplished.

goal is passion. To succeed, your vision must be something you feel strongly about. This should come through in your words and body language. Passion is contagious.

Getting people to buy in to your vision requires communicating on a level that is appropriate. You must consider who your audience is. Is it your peers, your neighbors, or local businesspeople whom you are trying to get to support your organization? When dealing with present and potential members of your group, you must consider what appeals to various types of people. Some people will be excited by the chance to accomplish something important and will respond well to the challenge of making it work. Some people are motivated by how others see them. They will work for a goal if they think it will make them look good to others and enhance their image. Others respond well to the social aspects of working with a group to accomplish something; they will join if they think working on the project will be fun. It's up to you to identify what motivates different people and emphasize those aspects of your project.

Establishing Goals

Whereas a vision is large and sweeping, goals are definite objectives that must be reached in order to achieve the vision. Having goals allows the leader and the team to measure their

Putting on a successful bake sale is often a short-range goal that moves a group closer to achieving a long-range goal that requires funds to accomplish.

progress. This makes it clear to the entire team exactly what must be done, when, and how. Goals can be long range or short range, and most endeavors require a mix of both. For example, a long-range goal might be to get new uniforms for a sports team by the start of the next school year. A short-range goal would then be to put on a successful bake sale to raise

some money toward this long-range goal. It is important to have long-range as well as short-range goals because long-range goals keep the team energized and focused when dealing with the practical efforts required to accomplish the short-range goals. In other words, this objective reminds people what they're working for and why. It can be important when short-term obstacles and frustrations arise.

The leader must engage the members of the group in establishing goals. It is important to get them to contribute ideas and to incorporate those ideas into the goals of the group. This serves two valuable purposes. Often, group members will have ideas that the leader has not thought of, and the members of the group will be more committed to working toward goals they view as "theirs" rather than "yours." Once goals are established, the leader and team members can come up with a series of specific tasks that must be accomplished to achieve each goal. People and resources are then assigned to each task, and team members set about working on them. Be aware, however, that by accepting the role of leader, you accept responsibility for seeing that the goals are accomplished—even if they were decided on by the group as a whole.

Quotations About Leadership

"If your actions inspire others to dream more, learn more, do more, and become more, you are a leader." —John Quincy Adams (1767–1848), sixth U.S. president

"Leadership should be born out of the understanding of the needs of those who would be affected by it." —Marian Anderson (1897–1993), American singer and civil rights activist

"The led must not be compelled; they must be able to choose their own leader." —Albert Einstein (1879–1955), Nobel Prize–winning physicist

"Leaders aren't born, they are made. And they're made just like anything else, through hard work. And that's the price we'll have to pay to achieve that goal, or any goal." —Vince Lombardi (1913–1970), American football coach

"Example is leadership." —Albert Schweitzer (1875–1965), physician and humanitarian

"The day soldiers stop bringing you their problems is the day you have stopped leading them. They have either lost confidence that you can help them or concluded that you do not care. Either case is a failure of leadership." —Colin Powell (1937–), former chairman of the Joint Chiefs of Staff and U.S. secretary of state

"Leadership is the art of getting someone else to do something you want done because he wants to do it." —Dwight D. Eisenhower (1890–1969), thirty-fourth U.S. president

"The task of a leader is to get his people from where they are to where they have not been." —Henry Kissinger (1923–), former U.S. secretary of state

"A leader is best when people barely know he exists. When his work is done, his aim fulfilled, they will say: 'We did it ourselves.'" —Lao Tzu (sixth century BCE), Chinese philosopher, *The Book of the Way*

Sources: "Leadership Quotes," retrieved March 27, 2011 (http://www.brainyquote.com/quotes/keywords/leadership.html); and Mark Shead, "Leadership Quotes," retrieved March 27, 2011 (http://www.leadership501.com/leadership-quotes/316).

Prioritizing

No matter how important the group and its goals are to you, it is only one part of your life. As a young person, you have to balance school, work, and home responsibilities. It is easy to take on too many responsibilities and become overwhelmed. This can lead to stress, which can cause physical and emotional problems. It is also easy to neglect aspects of your life that have long-term significance in order to pursue things that are more interesting or demand immediate attention, but that are of less importance in the long run. To avoid being overwhelmed and to focus on the aspects of your life that are most important, it is critical to prioritize your activities. First, you need to identify your responsibilities at home, school, and work. You also need to identify your personal goals. What do you want to do with your life? What do you want to achieve?

Next, you need to manage your time. Some of your responsibilities will be assigned, such as homework and chores. Others will be activities you want to do or that others, such as your friends, want you to do. You probably don't have time to do everything you want to

If you take on too many activities, ultimately you will not be able to do any well. Therefore, it is important to identify which are most important to you.

do or that others want you to do. So, you need to list the things you have to do in order of importance. How do you know which things are most important? Ask yourself the following questions about each item on your list:

1. Is this responsibility a matter of personal integrity (such as picking your little brother up after school when you promised to do so), or will it help me achieve one of my goals (such as doing your homework so that you can do well in school and go to college)?

2. Does it need to be done now? If not, when do I need to do it to get it done on time? (Schedule this on a calendar, smartphone, or computer.)

3. Can someone else do it? If you are a member of a group or team, there may be others who can perform the activity in question. This is called delegation.

Don't neglect personal health when you are considering your activities. For example, getting enough exercise helps you function in the best way possible, so make that a priority, too. Once you have your tasks in order, start on them, beginning with the most important. That way, if you can't do everything, as is likely, then you do the most important activities.

Another good question to ask about each task is whether there is a way to do it more efficiently or faster, without sacrificing quality. For example, if you needed to sell a box of candy bars to raise money for a school group, you could go door-to-door talking to individual neighbors, but it might be more efficient to go to the local mall and offer them to a large number of people all at once.

One very important point to remember is that priorities change over time. Therefore, they should be reviewed on a regular basis so that you can realign them, if necessary, to be sure you are always working toward your most important goals in all areas of your life.

CHAPTER 3

BUILDING TRUST

People will not follow a leader they don't trust, and they will follow one they do trust "to the ends of the Earth." Why is trust so important? The bottom line is that people follow a leader because they believe they can trust him or her to help them achieve their goals. Betray your followers or give them evidence that you are not trustworthy and you will lose them. Building trust requires making some hard choices at times, however.

Doing the Right Thing

Integrity is being true to yourself and your beliefs. It means standing up for what you believe is right and behaving in an honorable manner. Being charming may help you gain followers, but charm is not enough to make you a successful leader. If people find out that you are not trustworthy, they will abandon you just as fast as they joined you—and in today's world of instant information, it will take no time at all for your bad behavior to become public knowledge. There are several areas that will affect whether people view you as trustworthy or not.

One issue is: will you do what's right, rather than what's popular? For instance, if your friends engage in picking on or bullying those who are different, do you go along with it to retain your status in the group, or do you stand up for the weaker party? The former behavior may make you more popular with a small group, but it will make many people outside the clique turn away from you. If you are a leader in a group at the time you engage in such behavior, this may make many in the group believe that you will betray them if it comes to a choice between the group's interests and your own.

A second issue is cheating, whether it is cheating on a test or artificially enhancing your chances of winning at sports by taking steroids. Sooner or later, someone will find out about your behavior. Even if that person doesn't report you for your activity, he or she will tell others. If members of the group know you cheat in one area, they will expect you to do so in others. They will see you as someone who is unscrupulous, and they will believe that you will cheat them and the group if there is a benefit for you in doing so.

The reverse is also true. If you conduct yourself honestly and stand up for others when it is the right thing to do, group

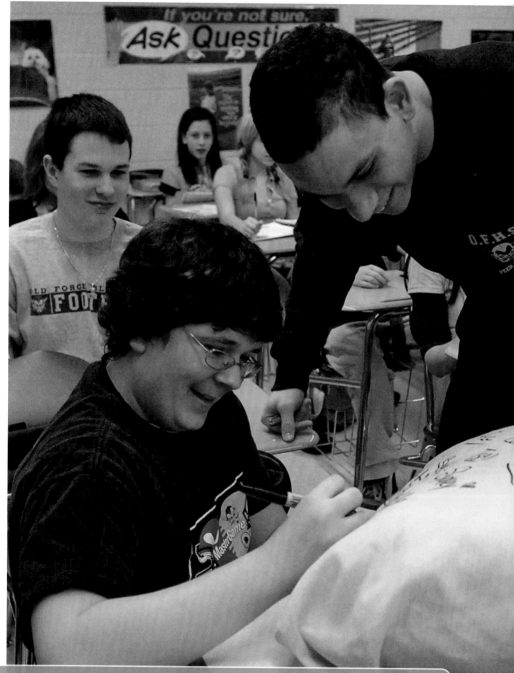

Students sign an antibullying pledge. Treating people who are different from you or who are less fortunate with respect can gain you respect in return.

members will come to view you as someone who will look out for the best interests
of individual group members and the group
as a whole. They will also see you as someone who is courageous and willing to fight for
what's right, which is sometimes necessary
for the group to achieve its goals. This type
of behavior is, therefore, a powerful motivator
when it comes to getting people to see you
as a leader.

Sharing Credit

One of the best ways to gain the trust of group
members is by making sure they get credit
for the group's accomplishments. Nothing
destroys the cohesion of a group faster than
the leader taking credit for the accomplishments of the group. Even if the group is
acting under the leader's direction, following his or her plan and vision, it is imperative
that the leader communicate to others that it
was the work and contributions of the people
in the group that led to its success. People
want to feel valued and important. Receiving
recognition from authority figures such as
coaches and teachers and from the larger
public—whether that is students and parents, or those who read the local newspaper

Seeing that group members get recognition for their efforts is a powerful way to motivate them to participate in future efforts and to believe in your leadership.

or a blog—gives group members a feeling of satisfaction. Seeing that group members get such recognition will make you a popular leader and make people work harder to achieve the group's goals.

Respect for Others

People have different skills, talents, and abilities. Some people are smarter than others, some are more artistic, and some are better athletes. This is especially true with volunteer groups, clubs, and class groups. However, all people have abilities that a leader can use. In any significant group activity, there are a variety of tasks that must be performed, from planning to setup and cleanup. A leader identifies the skills and ability levels of different people and sees that they are assigned to tasks they can do so that everyone can make a contribution. A true leader treats all people with respect and insists that other group members do so as well. He or she helps weaker members develop and make a contribution, rather than ridiculing them. Treating people with disrespect undermines the group's trust in the leader.

A true leader helps members develop and improve their skills. One way to do this is to pair inexperienced members with skilled ones so that they can learn.

Manipulation Is Not Leadership

Leaders learn to "read" people through their verbal and nonverbal communication and develop a sense of what will motivate them. Therefore, there are many situations in which a leader could use his or her understanding to manipulate people

to get what he or she wants. A leader does not manipulate people, even when they disagree with him or her or don't want to participate in an activity. For example, a leader who knows it's easy to make someone feel guilty won't make her feel guilty about not participating. Likewise, if someone is insecure, a leader will not force him to participate by implying that he's a wimp if he doesn't. Manipulating people not only makes them feel resentful but also creates fear in other members of the group that they may be a future target. These negative feelings make people less willing to participate and can lead people to quit the group.

10 Great Questions
TO ASK A TEACHER

1. How can I improve my written communication skills?

2. What books can I read that will improve my leadership skills?

3. Are there courses I can take to improve my communication and leadership skills?

4. Will you critique a speech I want to give about ideas for the group and tell me how I can improve it?

5. How do I deal with someone making trouble in the group?

6. How can I present myself well to local public officials and businesspeople?

7. What can I do to motivate group members who are not pulling their weight?

8. How can I improve my public speaking skills?

9. Does the school have resources I can use to prepare printed materials?

10. Does the school have audiovisual equipment I can use for presentations?

LEADING THE GROUP

Leading a group is not easy. Leaders have to make many decisions, sometimes unpopular ones. They have to deal with conflict within the group and keep the group moving forward to achieve its goals. They have to keep track of the group's progress toward achieving its goals and adjust plans when necessary to make sure the group succeeds. This chapter discusses some elements that make a leader successful in managing a group.

Leading by Example

The strongest type of communication is doing, not telling. True leaders inspire

Successful leaders participate in the work of the group as well as the planning. They show that they are willing to do the things they are asking others to do.

admiration and a desire to emulate them. This section discusses how to behave in a way that encourages others to follow your example. There is no such thing as "Do as I say, not as I do" when it comes to leadership. No matter what

you say, group members will pay attention to what you do. If you want people to work hard, treat each other with respect, and pull together, you must do the same. As soon as you ask people to behave one way and then act differently yourself, they will question your sincerity and think, "If you don't do that, why should I?"

Furthermore, behaving in the way you want other members of the group to behave provides a direct, practical example they can follow. Simply telling people to "Do this" isn't nearly as effective a teaching tool as a practical demonstration. Note that leading by example can work in a negative way as well. If you blame people when things go wrong instead of focusing on solving the problem in a constructive way, other members of the group will do the same. This leads to divisiveness and a desire to avoid bringing up potential problems. If, instead, you approach problems in a neutral fashion and get the team working on solutions, other members of the group will be more likely to work together to solve problems as well.

Brainstorming

Brainstorming is a technique for generating ideas on a specific subject. For instance, you might want to generate ideas for group activities, how to raise money, or how to solve a specific problem. There are many variations of the brainstorming process. The following steps detail one way it can be approached.

1. Start by getting as many people from the group together as possible. Having people with different points of view will lead to a wide variety of ideas.

2. State the issue or problem to be addressed as a clear, specific, open-ended question. For example, "How can we raise money to put on a play?" or "How can we get more people to join our group?"

3. Establish either a number or time limit. "We will collect seventy-five ideas" or "We will collect all the ideas we can in thirty minutes."

4. Have the group members call out or write down all the ideas they can think of until the established limit is reached. Write or copy them in a form everyone can see, for example, on a blackboard, whiteboard, or flip chart. Do not let anyone criticize or comment on the ideas. At this point, collect all the ideas no matter how absurd they seem. Criticism will stifle participation and creativity. The group will judge them later.

5. Establish a list of judging criteria, for example: an idea must be affordable within the group's finances or within their ability to raise enough money to accomplish; it must be possible to carry out the idea with the manpower available within the group; the idea must be acceptable to school authorities; an idea must be safe, and so on.

6. Discuss and rank the ideas. If the number of ideas is small, the pros and cons of each can be discussed. If there are a large number, you can have the group members rank them in order of importance. One way to do this is to have each group member give each idea a rank from 0–5. The ideas with the highest total scores are likely to be the best and have the most group support, so you can start by discussing the top five or ten ideas.

7. Obtain agreement on the best idea or ideas by a consensus (agreement among group members), voting, or ranking and scoring the ideas chosen for discussion.

Decisiveness and Flexibility

One of the important qualities of a leader is the ability to make decisions. Indecisiveness, vacillating between possible courses of action, is one of the biggest inhibitors of both individual and group success. Furthermore, indecisiveness creates an aura of weakness.

One factor that frequently stands in the way of making a decision is perfectionism, the belief that one must have the best possible solution or approach. A plan should not be sloppy. It should address the issues that need to be addressed. However, doing nothing for long periods of time, while searching for the perfect answer, is often less effective than doing something that will get the job done well, even if it isn't "perfect." It is important to understand that it is not necessary to have the "best" approach; it is usually sufficient to find an approach that will work and then execute it. This will get tasks done and goals achieved. A leader must be willing to make a choice among possible courses of action arrived at by the group and then stick to that choice— unless the situation itself changes. Continually changing course during a project wastes time and causes confusion. Sticking to the agreed-upon course often requires confidence on the part of the leader when problems arise. Group members may question whether the plan being followed is correct.

That being said, a leader must also be flexible. Situations often change, and new information can change assumptions that were made when the original plan was created. When adjusting the original plan would be appropriate for legitimate reasons, a good leader does not stubbornly insist that the

An important responsibility of a leader is obtaining feedback from group members to evaluate how well the group's projects are going and adjusting course if necessary.

group stick to it. A leader needs to assess the group's progress from time to time, decide whether the approach being taken is still correct, and make adjustments when necessary. Thus, leadership requires balancing decisiveness and flexibility.

Encouraging Creativity

It is important to encourage group members to be creative, both in developing activities and in solving problems. One key to encouraging creativity is to foster an atmosphere that is

53

nonjudgmental. It should not be acceptable for either the leader or the group members to shoot down another person's ideas until the person has been heard out or to discourage a person from trying something new that he or she feels might work. It is often very difficult to get others to accept an idea that differs from the way things have been done in the past. One of the roles of a leader is to make sure that new ideas that may benefit the group get a fair trial.

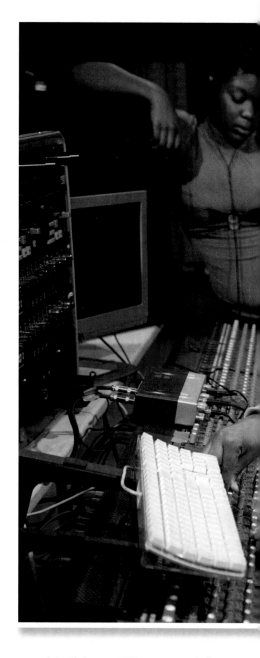

Another way to foster creativity is to let people take responsibility for activities without micromanaging how they accomplish them. Someone might not tackle a task in the same way you would, but you must give people the freedom to accomplish tasks in their own way. Nothing stifles creativity as fast as the leader insisting that everything be done his or her

A group of students use a sound mixer. Trying new ideas often leads to unexpected solutions to problems or improved techniques. An environment in which people feel safe trying new things is essential.

way. The leader should interfere only if the task is not being done or if the person to whom it is delegated asks for assistance. The same is true of problems. If a problem arises with an activity, give the person responsible for the task, or the group as a whole, the chance to come up with ways to solve the problem before telling them what to do. Equally important is to recognize people when they come up with a creative idea or solution that works. Nothing fosters future creativity like acknowledging people's successes.

Dealing with Conflict

Every leader has to deal with conflict in the group. People sometimes have habits that irritate other team members, are unnecessarily negative, or are disruptive. Among young people, conflicts are even more common than among adult employees because (1) they are still figuring out their place in the "pecking order" and may pick on those who are different or less talented, (2) they may have less well-developed coping skills when things go wrong, and (3) they may be insecure and fear being blamed for problems, among other things. This section discusses ways to deal with conflicts in the group.

A teenage facilitator helps kids understand how people perceive their enemies. Such processes help reduce conflict between people with different backgrounds and views.

One type of confrontation occurs between two people who start picking on each other or arguing. It's easier to stop such confrontations before they get out of control. If a person in the group starts making nasty remarks to another, try to put a stop to it immediately. You might say something like, "Come

When people have differences of opinion or issues with each other, sometimes a neutral person talking with all of them can assist them in arriving at a compromise.

on, we're all trying to work on this, OK? Let's not get personal." If you have laid out a set of standards for behavior in the group, such as "Everyone will be treated with respect," you can remind the offenders that they agreed to behave in that way. Often, one can use humor to defuse a tense situation, but be sure not to make fun of either party in the confrontation. If possible, take the people involved to a separate room and discuss the problem with them. Act as a mediator, a neutral person who listens to both sides of the story and helps the two people arrive at a mutually satisfactory solution.

Never get between two people who are having a confrontation because this could be dangerous if things get physical. If you think a confrontation might turn violent, have everyone else leave the room or area and find a teacher or other authority, explain the situation, and have him or her deal with the problem. Everyone simply walking out may cause those having the confrontation to stop out of embarrassment.

Other types of conflict may be subtler but still damaging to group cohesion. Sometimes a person will try to lord it over other group members, showing off and putting others down. This person may actually be making significant contributions to the group and reveling in being a superstar—or he or she may just be obnoxious. In this type of situation, having a private talk with the person may help. Tell the person you recognize the contributions he or she is making. However, point out that his or her behavior is demoralizing other members of the group, and this is hurting the group's chances of accomplishing what it's trying to do. Point out that the person obviously cares about accomplishing the group's goals, or he or she wouldn't be making such an effort, and then ask for his or her assistance with the others in the group. Appealing to the superstar's ego in this way can sometimes turn the person from a problem into an asset.

One of the most difficult problems to deal with in a group is a negative person. Some individuals seem to see the downside of everything and are quick to point out that whatever is suggested won't work. This attitude can suck the life out of a group. One approach to dealing with such people is to prevent them from infusing every meeting or task with their negative viewpoint. Acknowledge that what they say might—or might not—turn out to be true, then ask them what they think is positive about the plan or task. If they refuse to respond, immediately ask other group members what they see as positive. This turns the conversation into a dialog with differing viewpoints, not a negative statement of fact that should be accepted.

Although no one approach works all the time, across the board, one of the most successful approaches to dealing with problem people is to redirect them. Sit down, talk to them, and ask them to help you with the group, a task, or solving a problem. Make them feel important and needed, since they are often seeking attention or are insecure and isolated and are trying to impress people. Having a vested interest in the success of a project, and feeling valued, can often turn their behavior from destructive to constructive.

CHAPTER 5

DEVELOPING AS A LEADER

A true leader keeps developing both personal strengths and knowledge. Leadership is a process. The more you learn and practice, the greater your skills become. This section talks about ways a leader can improve existing skills and develop new ones.

Gaining Confidence

A leader must be confident. If you don't believe you are capable of shouldering the burdens of leadership, neither will anyone else. You do not need to have the answer

Accepting challenges helps develop confidence that one can overcome obstacles and achieve goals. Having confidence in yourself is a major factor in your ability to lead.

to every question or the solution to every problem that arises. There are many other group members who can help you come up with specific solutions. However, you do need to know that you are capable of dealing with questions and problems when they arise. You need to believe that you can keep members of the group cooperating in an orderly fashion and keep them from panicking. One of the major reasons people look upon someone as a leader is that he or she remains calm and approaches problem solving in an orderly fashion. This makes people view the leader as strong and secure, someone who can be depended upon.

Many people think they are displaying confidence by constantly stating or demonstrating how smart or skilled they are. This makes others feel inferior and intimidates them. It is also likely to make them want to stay away from the leader, not follow him or her. Therefore, it is necessary to learn how to communicate confidence in a way that inspires, not offends, people. Show your confidence by what you do, not by talking about how great you are.

How do you develop this confidence? By putting yourself in situations that challenge you and seeing them through. There is no substitute for seeing a challenge through to the end, to convince yourself that you can survive other challenges. You do not have to succeed in every challenge. Many great leaders have failed along the way. However, they saw the challenge through, survived the failures, and then went on to the next challenge. That is the type of self-confidence that defines a leader.

Mentoring

A mentor is a person with expertise who is willing to provide one-on-one guidance and support. A mentor can help you develop leadership skills faster, help you steer clear of mistakes, and provide you with advice when you run into problems. A mentor can be a coach, a teacher, or a professional in a field you are interested in. He or she could be an older family member or family friend. Find a person whose leadership and communication expertise you respect. Explain to this person that you are leading a group, and ask if he or she would be willing to act as your mentor. Be sure to explain why you chose him or her and what sorts of things you'd like help with. If that person can't help you, perhaps because of other commitments, don't be discouraged. Simply try another person you admire. The first person you ask may even be able to refer you to someone else who can help.

If your chosen mentor agrees, communicate with him or her regularly to discuss the activities you are involved in and the issues you are dealing with. You can meet face-to-face, perhaps weekly or monthly, or you can maintain an e-mail correspondence. Remember that your mentor is giving you advice, not orders. You should evaluate your mentor's suggestions and decide if all or some of them are right for the situation. There will be times when you disagree with what your mentor suggests. A mentor is giving you the benefit of his or her experience. Your group or situation may be different from what he or she is familiar with. The goal of having a mentor is developing the ability to manage on your own. So, the decision on what advice to accept is yours.

Give your mentor feedback; share what worked and what didn't. Above all, show gratitude to your mentor. Express your thanks for his or her help.

Continuing to Learn

Leadership is not a single set of skills one learns and then proceeds to apply. The better a leader's skills are in all aspects of management, communication, and leadership techniques, the more effective he or she will be. Areas worth studying include fund-raising, public speaking, composition, project planning, and accounting/financial management, among others. Having good computer skills is useful as well. New approaches and techniques for managing and communicating are continuously being developed. New tools such as project management software are also being developed. So, staying current on these tools and techniques can make your job as a leader easier. Reading print or online magazines on management can provide you with information

on techniques you could add to your repertoire of leadership tools. Be sure to critically evaluate such techniques before you adopt them, however. Make sure they are appropriate and ethical.

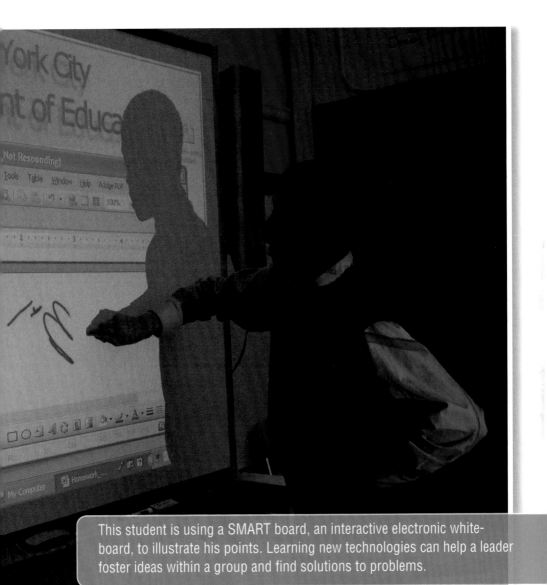

This student is using a SMART board, an interactive electronic white-board, to illustrate his points. Learning new technologies can help a leader foster ideas within a group and find solutions to problems.

A leader is a lifelong learner, and not just about leadership techniques. The best leaders have a wide range of general knowledge covering many subjects. In the course of leading a group, generating ideas, and solving problems, you will benefit from knowledge of many different areas. History, literature, mathematics, science, psychology, languages, the arts, and other subjects can all provide information of use as a leader. People who can look at a problem from a variety of perspectives often see solutions that are missed by those whose training is too narrow. Therefore, leaders should take every opportunity to read and study and keep learning, even after they are finished with school.

The fact is that the best leaders are always hungry for more knowledge and more practice. They are constantly learning, and what they learn gives them the tools to excel.

GLOSSARY

ABUNDANCE A plentiful or sufficient amount.

ACTIVE LISTENING A method of attending to what others say that ensures one hears and understands their meaning.

AMBIGUITY An expression or statement that has more than one meeting; a situation in which something can be understood in more than one way and it is not clear which meaning is intended.

ARTICULATE Capable of communicating in a clear and well-organized way.

AURA Atmosphere that surrounds a person or object.

BIAS Prejudice in favor of or against one thing, person, or group compared with another, usually considered to be unfair.

BODY LANGUAGE Communication through conscious or subconscious hand gestures, facial expressions, and other body movements; also called nonverbal communication.

CLIQUE A small and exclusive group of people.

COHESION Sticking together.

COMPELLING Holding attention or attracting strong interest.

CONSENSUS Agreement among a group of people.

CONSTRUCTIVE Productive or useful.

CRITERIA Rules or standards for judging something.

CRITIQUE A review of someone's work.

DEFUSE To reduce the danger or tension in a difficult situation.

DELEGATE To appoint someone else to carry out a task or function.

DEMORALIZE To destroy the courage, confidence, or hope of a person or group.

DIVISIVE Causing disunity.

EARMARK To designate something for a particular purpose.

EMPATHY The ability to understand and share the feelings of another person.

EMULATE To model oneself after, try to be like.

ENDEAVOR An undertaking.

ETHICAL The morally correct or right behavior.

HOMONYMS Words that sound the same but have different meanings, such as "bear" and "bare."

HOSPITABLE Welcoming.

IMPERATIVE Of vital importance; crucial.

INDECISIVE Unable to make up one's mind.

INFUSE To fill; to instill a quality in someone or something.

INHIBIT To block.

INTEGRITY Being true to one's beliefs, honest, and honorable.

INTIMIDATE To frighten.

JARGON Terms used by a particular group that may not be understood by those outside the group.

LEGITIMATE True to established principles.

MICROMANAGE To tell people how to do the details of their job.

MOTIVATE To inspire.

PARAMOUNT Of utmost importance.

PARAPHRASE To rephrase something in one's own words.

PERSEVERANCE Persistence, staying on a course of action despite obstacles.

PROOFREAD To read something that is written and mark any errors in it.

REALIGN To change one's position or attitude to fit different circumstances.

REFERENDUM A vote by a whole population on an issue.

REPERTOIRE A collection of skills and techniques.

STIFLE To smother.

UNSCRUPULOUS Unprincipled, dishonest.

VACILLATE To waver back and forth.

FOR MORE INFORMATION

American Management Association
1601 Broadway
New York, NY 10019
(877) 566-9441 or (212) 903-8392
Web site: http://www.amanet.org
This organization provides books, seminars, and other resources on
    management. It offers a student membership.

J-Teen Leadership
701 Westchester Avenue, Suite 203E
White Plains, NY 10604
(914) 328-8788
Web site: http://www.jteenleadership.org
The organization empowers Jewish teens from all backgrounds with
    leadership training.

Kiwanis Key-Leader
3636 Woodview Trace
Indianapolis, IN 46268
(800) 549-2647, ext. 124
Web site: http://www.key-leader.org
This is a program of Kiwanis International that offers leadership
    resources and programs for teens.

National 4-H Council
7100 Connecticut Avenue
Chevy Chase, MD 20815
(301) 961-2800
Web site: http://www.4-h.org
This organization provides programs to develop practical skills and
    leadership capabilities in young people.

National Teen Leadership Program
101 Parkshore Drive
Folsom, CA 95630
(800) 550-1950
Web site: http://www.ntlp.org
This organization provides leadership programs for teens, including
    summer and one-day programs.

Teen Leadership Corps
26 East Cedar Point Road
Sandusky, OH 44870
(419) 621-5426
Web site: http://www.teenleadershipcorps.com
This organization provides an opportunity for teens to learn leadership
    skills through involvement in community service.

Teen Leadership Foundation
1280 Bison Avenue, B9-115
Newport Beach, CA 92660
(949) 769-6670
Web site: http://www.teenleadershipfoundation.org
This organization provides leadership programs for at-risk teens.

Web Sites

Due to the changing nature of Internet links, Rosen Publishing
has developed an online list of Web sites related to the subject
of this book. This site is updated regularly. Please use this link
to access this list:

http://www.rosenlinks.com/cwc/lead

FOR FURTHER READING

Aikins, Anne Marie. *Misconduct: Deal with It Without Bending the Rules*. Davidson, NC: Lorimer, 2005.

Baker, Jed. *Social Skills Picture Book for High School and Beyond*. Arlington, TX: Future Horizons Press, 2006.

Bordessa, Kris. *Team Challenges: 170+ Group Activities to Build Cooperation, Communication, and Creativity*. Chicago, IL: Zephyr Press, 2005.

Bradberry, Travis, Jean Greaves, and Patrick M. Lencioni. *Emotional Intelligence 2.0*. San Diego, CA: TalentSmart, 2009.

Burns, James MacGregor. *Transforming Leadership*. New York, NY: Grove Press, 2004.

Esherick, Joan. *Balancing Act: A Teen's Guide to Managing Stress*. Broomall, PA: Mason Crest Publishers, 2005.

Facts On File, Inc. *Communication Skills* (Career Skills Library). New York, NY: Infobase Publishing, 2009.

Judson, Karen. *Resolving Conflicts: How to Get Along When You Don't Get Along*. Berkeley Heights, NJ: Enslow Publishers, 2005.

Kahaner, Ellen. *Great Communication Skills* (Work Readiness). New York, NY: Rosen Publishing, 2008.

Kouzes, James M., and Barry Z. Posner. *The Five Practices of Exemplary Student Leadership: A Brief Introduction*. San Francisco, CA: Jossey-Bass, 2005.

Kouzes, James M., and Barry Z. Posner. *The Student Leadership Challenge: Five Practices for Exemplary Leaders*. San Francisco, CA: Jossey-Bass, 2008.

Kouzes, James M., and Barry Z. Posner. *Student Leadership Planner: An Action Guide to Achieving Your Personal Best*. San Francisco: Jossey-Bass, 2005.

MacGregor, Mariam G. *Everyday Leadership: Attitudes and Actions for Respect and Success* (A Guidebook for Teens). Minneapolis, MN: Free Spirit Publishing, 2006.

MacKay, Matthew. *The Communication Skills Book*. Oakland, CA: New Harbinger Publications, 2009.

McCollum, Sean, and Madonna M. Murphy. *Managing Conflict Resolution*. New York, NY: Chelsea House Publishers, 2009.

Nelson, Bob, and Peter Economy. *Managing for Dummies*. Hoboken, NJ: Wiley Publishing, 2010.

Shankman, Marcy L., and Scott J. Allen. *Emotionally Intelligent Leadership for Students Development Guide*. San Francisco, CA: Jossey-Bass, 2010.

Sommers, Michael. *Great Interpersonal Skills* (Work Readiness). New York, NY: Rosen Publishing, 2008.

Sprenger, B. Marilee. *The Leadership Brain for Dummies*. Hoboken, NJ: Wiley Publishing, 2010.

Strunk, William, Jr., and E. B. White. *The Elements of Style*. Ithaca, NY: BN Publishing, 2007.

BIBLIOGRAPHY

All Business. *"Ten Ways to Improve Your Interpersonal Skills."* Retrieved February 5, 2011 (http://www.allbusiness.com/human-resources/careers-career-development/11134-1.html).

Baumgartner, Jeffrey. *"The Step-by-Step Guide to Brainstorming."* JPD.com. Retrieved February 22, 2011 (http://www.jpb.com/creative/brainstorming.php).

Burns, Karen. *"On Careers: 13 Tips for Finding a Mentor."* U.S. News, January 13, 2010. Retrieved February 22, 2011 (http://money.usnews.com/money/blogs/outside-voices-careers/2010/01/13/13-tips-on-finding-a-mentor).

College Board. *"Time Management Tips for Students."* Retrieved February 17, 2011 (http://www.collegeboard.com/student/plan/college-success/116.html).

CompanyofExperts.net. *"For Leaders: Sixteen Ways of Developing Empathy."* Retrieved February 26, 2011 (http://www.companyofexperts.net/biz/2009/08/18/for-leaders-sixteen-ways-of-developing-empathy).

Free Management Library. *"All About Teambuilding."* Retrieved February 18, 2011 (http://managementhelp.org/grp_skll/teams/teams.htm).

Inc.com. *"Better Communication with Employees and Peers."* Retrieved February 14, 2011 (http://www.inc.com/guides/growth/23032.html).

Kouzes, James M., and Barry Z. Posner. *The Truth About Leadership.* San Francisco, CA; Jossey-Bass, 2010.

Learning Center. *"How to Build a Team."* Retrieved February 19, 2011 (http://www.learningcenter.net/library/building.shtml).

Maxell, John. *Teamwork 101.* Nashville, TN: Maxwell Motivation, 2009.

MindTools. *"Active Listening."* Retrieved February 7, 2011 (http://www.mindtools.com/CommSkll/ActiveListening.htm).

MindTools. *"Conflict Resolution."* Retrieved February 20, 2011 (http://www.mindtools.com/pages/article/newLDR_81.htm).

Rye, David. *Stop Managing and Lead*. Avon, MA: Adams Press, 2009.

Southern Georgia University Center for Leadership. *"The Importance of Good Listening Skills."* The Eagle Banner Leadership Series. No. 8. Retrieved February 23, 2011 (http://students.georgiasouthern.edu/leadership/documents/banners/2005%20Eagle%20Banner%20march%20-%20GoodListening Skills-Mar.05.pdf).

INDEX

About the Author

Jeri Freedman has a B.A. from Harvard University. She is the author of more than thirty young adult nonfiction books, including *First Bank Account and First Investments*, *Careers in Computer Science and Programming*, and *Women in the Workplace: Wages, Respect, and Equal Rights*.

Photo Credits